STICKER
SPOT
IT

:BIRDS

Written by Rachael Elizabeth Conisbee
Illustrated by Repro India Ltd

UK

ing plc

HOW TO USE YOUR SPOT IT GUIDE

Next time you are awoken by the dawn chorus, why not look outside? Open your eyes wide to discover all about the beautiful birds around you! There are 101 different types to spot.

Firstly, have fun attaching the specially-shaped stickers onto the outlines on some of the pages. There are matching numbers to help you.

When you've spotted something, stick in one of the round stickers, and make a note of when, and where, you saw it.

We've also rated the birds according to how likely you are to see them. Ten points means you've spotted and scored an easy target while 60 points means you've found a really rare type! How long will it take you to reach the maximum score of 3,560?

HINTS AND TIPS

- Why not join a nature walk? Many birds build their nests in tree branches and trunks.
- Ask an adult to accompany you to a river or pond to see birds that live by the water.
- Remember – whether you see the bird for real, on the Internet, in books, or magazines – they all count as 'Spots'!

NAME: Canada goose

DESCRIPTION: These birds are very tame, nesting at the water's edge or on an island. They stay in Britain throughout the year. The females lay around five creamy-white eggs in April/May. They can be identified by their trumpet-like honking which can be heard when the birds are flying low across the countryside. They have a black head and white chin. **POINTS VALUE:** 20

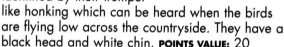

| DATE SPOTTED: | SPOT IT! | GOT IT! |
| WHERE SPOTTED: | | |

NAME: Greylag goose

DESCRIPTION: The largest and bulkiest geese native to Britain, they breed around parkland lakes and reservoirs, and can be seen, or heard, making a loud, cackling sound, in lowland areas throughout the year. Their young goslings can fly after two months, although stay with their family for several months before setting off on their own. **POINTS VALUE:** 30

| DATE SPOTTED: | SPOT IT! | GOT IT! |
| WHERE SPOTTED: | | |

NAME: Pink-footed goose

DESCRIPTION: These small, grey geese have dark heads and necks. Their bills, feet and legs are pink. They don't breed in Britain, but visit us for the winter months from colder climates such as Iceland and Greenland. Their call is high-pitched and shrill. As well as eating grain and cereals, they also enjoy eating potatoes! **POINTS VALUE:** 50

DATE SPOTTED:

WHERE SPOTTED:

SPOT IT!   GOT IT!

NAME: Mute swan

DESCRIPTION: These white swans are graceful and pretty, but have a quarrelsome nature. They bully smaller swans, and hiss and snort when angry. They have bright orange bills and huge wings, which make a loud, throbbing hum in flight. You can find mute swans on lakes, rivers and ponds, in parks and across the countryside. Their favourite foods include insects and snails. **POINTS VALUE:** 20

DATE SPOTTED:

WHERE SPOTTED:

SPOT IT!   GOT IT!

4

NAME: Bewick's swan

DESCRIPTION: These are the smallest of British swans, with short necks and round heads. They have small, yellow patches on their bills. By coming to Britain from Siberia for the winter, they can enjoy eating leaves, shoots and roots. These swans are often seen with their tails sticking out of the water, with their heads deep underwater, feeding on the bottom of rivers and lakes. **POINTS VALUE:** 40

DATE SPOTTED:

WHERE SPOTTED:

SPOT IT!   **GOT IT!**

NAME: Whooper swan

DESCRIPTION: Whooper swans are noisy birds, with a call that sounds like a trumpet. They have long, thin necks and black legs. They visit us from Iceland for the winter, and lay 3–5 eggs. Unlike other swans, the whooper can often be seen grazing on river banks with the rest of their family, but you may also see them swimming on lakes, or flooded fields. **POINTS VALUE:** 40

DATE SPOTTED:

WHERE SPOTTED:

SPOT IT!   **GOT IT!**

NAME: Mallard

DESCRIPTION: These are 'dabbling' ducks that feed on the surface of the water. The females have broad, flat, green-yellow bills, and blue wing patches, while the males can be identified by their glossy green heads and curly, black tail feathers. Female mallards quack while males remain quiet, giving an occasional call when suspicious or frightened. **POINTS VALUE:** 10

DATE SPOTTED:

WHERE SPOTTED:

SPOT IT! GOT IT!

· ·

NAME: Shoveler

DESCRIPTION: Shovelers have long, rounded, spade-like bills, useful for sifting large volumes of water for food particles. They eat seeds, insects and tadpoles, using tiny teeth inside their bills to trap food. The males have green heads and white breasts, whereas the females are brown and speckled. They are quiet ducks; the males sometimes make a low-pitched 'took took' noise when flying. **POINTS VALUE:** 30

DATE SPOTTED:

WHERE SPOTTED:

SPOT IT! GOT IT!

NAME: Great-crested grebe

DESCRIPTION: These are water birds with ornate head plumes. Young grebes often travel on their parents' backs until they can swim for themselves. **POINTS VALUE:** 30

DATE SPOTTED:

WHERE SPOTTED:

SPOT IT! GOT IT!

· ·

NAME: Little grebe

DESCRIPTION: These are the smallest, most common grebes in Britain. They have fluffy rear ends, and in summer, bright chestnut-coloured throats. They are expert divers, often going underwater and reappearing great distances away. These grebes can be identified by their call that sounds like the whinnying of a horse. They live near slow moving water. **POINTS VALUE:** 20

DATE SPOTTED:

WHERE SPOTTED:

SPOT IT! GOT IT!

· ·

NAME: Black-necked grebe

DESCRIPTION: These birds live near large water expanses, lush with vegetation. They have golden tufts sprouting from either side of their head, and black heads and necks. **POINTS VALUE:** 60

DATE SPOTTED:

WHERE SPOTTED:

SPOT IT! GOT IT!

7

NAME: Bittern

DESCRIPTION: Bitterns are thick-set, with bright, pale brown plumage covered with dark streaks and bars. They have broad, rounded wings, and are difficult to see because they move silently through the reeds at the edge of water, in search of fish. They have a deep call that can be heard from as far away as one mile, which sounds like the bellowing of a bull. **POINTS VALUE:** 50

DATE SPOTTED: SPOT IT!   GOT IT!

WHERE SPOTTED:

NAME: Grey heron

DESCRIPTION: Grey herons nest in colonies, building in large trees, bushes or cliff edges, using the same nests year after year. They are large, long legged, and have a black-crested white head with dark streaks down their necks. When herons fly, they draw their neck into their body and extend their legs well beyond their tails. Herons eat fish and small mammals, and stab their prey with their razor-sharp bill, before swallowing their catch whole. **POINTS VALUE:** 40

DATE SPOTTED: SPOT IT!   GOT IT!

WHERE SPOTTED:

NAME: Crane

DESCRIPTION: Cranes are larger than other herons, and carry their bodies more horizontally. They are mainly grey with long legs and a long neck, and have drooping, curved tail feathers. They pass through Britain during spring and autumn on their way to warmer climates. Cranes eat seeds, crops, insects, snails and worms. They have a loud, clanging, trumpet-like call.

POINTS VALUE: 60

DATE SPOTTED:

WHERE SPOTTED:

SPOT IT! GOT IT!

. . . .

NAME: Spoonbill

DESCRIPTION: Spoonbills are tall, white, water birds, with long black bills shaped like spoons at the end, and long black legs. In water they sweep their bill from side to side to trap food such as small fish and insects. Some adults have yellow breasts during the mating season. They are very rare. They spend their time in Africa but a few stay in Britain all year round. They are best spotted in estuaries or coastal lagoons. **POINTS VALUE:** 60

DATE SPOTTED:

WHERE SPOTTED:

SPOT IT! GOT IT!

NAME: Moorhen

DESCRIPTION: Moorhen are medium-sized, ground-dwelling birds normally found by water. From a distance they look black; but get closer and you'll see they are actually olive-brown. They have bright red bills and foreheads, and long toes which give them a strange swimming style. Moorhens are good underwater swimmers and can stay underwater if alarmed, with just their bill sticking out.

POINTS VALUE: 10

DATE SPOTTED:

WHERE SPOTTED:

SPOT IT! ✓ GOT IT!

NAME: Coot

DESCRIPTION: Coots are jet black with brilliant white bills and have small, bald patches on their foreheads. They have flaps between their toes, which make their feet into webs, and this helps them to swim and dive. They can run short distances across the top of water, making a loud sploshing noise. They love lakes, ponds and rivers – and like to eat snails!

POINTS VALUE: 20

DATE SPOTTED:

WHERE SPOTTED:

SPOT IT! GOT IT!

NAME: Corncrake

DESCRIPTION: Corncrakes live on dry land and are very secretive and hard to find. When flying, they show off their bright chestnut wings, and trail their legs behind them. They also have distinctive striped bellies.

POINTS VALUE: 60

DATE SPOTTED:

WHERE SPOTTED:

SPOT IT!   GOT IT!

. . . .

NAME: Spotted crake

DESCRIPTION: Spotted crakes are slightly smaller than water rails, with short orange/yellow bills, white spots on their throats and greenish legs. Although good swimmers, spotted crakes rarely cross large stretches of water, preferring to fly. **POINTS VALUE:** 60

DATE SPOTTED:

WHERE SPOTTED:

SPOT IT!   GOT IT!

. . . .

NAME: Water rail

DESCRIPTION: These birds are smaller and slimmer than the moorhen. The best time to see them is in winter. They have brown and black upper bodies, grey faces and lower bodies, and black and white striped sides. They have a long red bill, and enjoy eating small fish and insects. **POINTS VALUE:** 30

DATE SPOTTED:

WHERE SPOTTED:

SPOT IT!   GOT IT!

NAME: Oystercatcher

DESCRIPTION: Oystercatchers are large, black and white wading birds, with long orange/red bills and pink legs. They have white wing stripes that are revealed when they fly, and white rumps in the shape of a V between their wings. They live near the seashore, and eat all kinds of seafood – mussels, cockles, small crabs and shrimps. **POINTS VALUE:** 20

DATE SPOTTED:

WHERE SPOTTED:

SPOT IT! GOT IT!

. . . .

NAME: Grey plover

DESCRIPTION: This delicate bird breeds in Canada and Russia and visits Britain in autumn/winter, although a few stay for the summer. They live in groups of two/three, and can be seen searching the seashore for food. They are grey in the winter, and black in summer.

POINTS VALUE: 30

DATE SPOTTED:

WHERE SPOTTED:

SPOT IT! GOT IT!

NAME: Lapwing

DESCRIPTION: Lapwings can be seen all year round on farmland and meadows. They are also known as the 'peewit' as this is the sound they make when calling. They have greenish-black plumage, white undersides and long crests of feathers coming from the back of their heads. Lapwings enjoy diving, twisting and rolling through the air.

POINTS VALUE: 10

DATE SPOTTED:

WHERE SPOTTED:

SPOT IT!   GOT IT!

- -

NAME: Dunlin

DESCRIPTION: These small birds are found in Britain all year round. At high tide, huge flocks fly along the shore, looking like a cloud of smoke from a distance. When they are breeding, you will see their slightly down-turned bills and black belly patches. They use their long bills to probe into the sand (like a sewing machine) when looking for their food.

POINTS VALUE: 10

DATE SPOTTED:

WHERE SPOTTED:

SPOT IT!   GOT IT!

NAME: Razorbill

DESCRIPTION: These medium- sized seabirds have black upper bodies and white bellies. Their thick, black beaks are razor sharp and hooked at the end, making it easier to catch fish and protect themselves against enemies. Before breeding, groups of razorbills perform a spectacular mass diving display in the sea. **POINTS VALUE:** 40

DATE SPOTTED:

WHERE SPOTTED:

SPOT IT!   GOT IT!

NAME: Common gull

DESCRIPTION: These small gulls have greeny-yellow legs and yellow bills. They are mainly found on the coast, though some can be seen in towns in the winter. They can be seen all year round – in the winter they like to nest further inland where it is warmer, and get their food by picking up insects found in furrowed fields. **POINTS VALUE:** 20

DATE SPOTTED:

WHERE SPOTTED:

SPOT IT!   GOT IT!

NAME: Arctic tern

DESCRIPTION: Terns have short, red legs, red bills, white bodies and black heads. They live along the British coastline from May to September and often nest on islands to avoid predators. **POINTS VALUE:** 40

DATE SPOTTED:

SPOT IT!   GOT IT!

WHERE SPOTTED:

NAME: Common tern

DESCRIPTION: Common terns are silvery-grey and white, and have long tails. Their bills are red with black tips. They hover over water before diving in to catch fish, and can be seen flying back to their nests with fish in their bills. **POINTS VALUE:** 40

DATE SPOTTED:

WHERE SPOTTED: SPOT IT!   GOT IT!

NAME: Kingfisher

DESCRIPTION: These shy birds fly low along riverbanks all year round. They are blue/green with orange underbodies, and white throats and neck patches. They have long, dagger-like bills, which are useful for catching fish and insects. Kingfishers have a distinctive call, which is shrill and loud, sounding like 'cheeeee'. **POINTS VALUE:** 40

DATE SPOTTED: SPOT IT! ✔   GOT IT!

WHERE SPOTTED:

15

NAME: Green woodpecker

DESCRIPTION: These are the largest woodpeckers in Britain. They have green backs and the tops of their heads are bright red. Their tails are short, and they can often be seen perching on a branch in the water near meadows, woods and parks. They make their nests in the bottom of tree trunks or in large branches, and stay in their nests for most of the winter. They eat insects and ants. **POINTS VALUE:** 40

DATE SPOTTED: SPOT IT!   GOT IT!
WHERE SPOTTED:

- -

NAME: Great spotted woodpecker

DESCRIPTION: These are black and white birds with red feathers under their tails. Males have a red patch on their heads. They nest in old tree trunks, and love to eat food put out for them by humans in the woods, but also eat insects and seeds. They make a fast drumming sound with their bills on tree trunks. **POINTS VALUE:** 30

DATE SPOTTED: SPOT IT!   GOT IT!
WHERE SPOTTED:

NAME: Goldcrest

DESCRIPTION: Goldcrests are the smallest songbird in Britain. They have dull, green backs and white bellies, with bright yellow/orange stripes on their heads – like that of a Mohican hairstyle. They live in forests with lots of conifer trees, though are sometimes seen in parks and large gardens. They live in Britain all year round.

POINTS VALUE: 10

DATE SPOTTED:

WHERE SPOTTED:

SPOT IT!   GOT IT!

· ·

NAME: Treecreeper

DESCRIPTION: Treecreepers have long claws and long, stiff tails which help them creep jerkily up tree trunks. Once at the top, they fly to the bottom of the next tree and begin to climb again. They eat beetles, moths, woodlice, spiders and other insects. Their bills curve down which helps them to catch insects. They are speckled brown with white bellies and white eyebrows.

POINTS VALUE: 20

DATE SPOTTED:

WHERE SPOTTED:

SPOT IT!   GOT IT!

NAME: Waxwing

DESCRIPTION: These plump birds are red/brown with black throats and small black masks around their eyes. The tips of their tails are yellow and they have red tips on the end of their wing feathers, like blobs of wax. They do not breed in Britain but visit in the winter where they stay in parks or gardens, and eat berries. **POINTS VALUE:** 60

DATE SPOTTED:　　　　　　　　　SPOT IT!　　GOT IT!

WHERE SPOTTED:

NAME: Wren

DESCRIPTION: These tiny, brown birds are almost round, with fine bills, long legs and toes, and very short round wings. Their narrow tails stick straight upwards, making wrens easy to identify. They are very common in Britain and nest in all sorts of places, including garden sheds and hedgerows. They have very loud voices that are shrill and repetitive. **POINTS VALUE:** 10

DATE SPOTTED:　　　　　　　　　SPOT IT!　　GOT IT!

WHERE SPOTTED:

NAME: Dunnock

DESCRIPTION: Dunnocks are small, brown and grey songbirds with warbling voices. They are most at home hopping along flower beds or near bushes, in search of insects and worms.

POINTS VALUE: 10

DATE SPOTTED:	SPOT IT!	GOT IT!
WHERE SPOTTED:		

NAME: Dipper

DESCRIPTION: Dippers have dark upper bodies, and white chests and throats. Their constant habit of bobbing up and down make them easy to spot. They are able to walk under water in search of food.

POINTS VALUE: 30

DATE SPOTTED:	SPOT IT!	GOT IT!
WHERE SPOTTED:		

NAME: Whitethroat

DESCRIPTION: Whitethroats have long tails, which they flick and tilt upwards as they dive in and out of hedgerows. They have grey heads and brown backs, with buff bellies and white throats. They visit for the summer from Africa, and like sunny, open areas with lots of cover such as brambles and bushes.

POINTS VALUE: 30

DATE SPOTTED:	SPOT IT!	GOT IT!
WHERE SPOTTED:		

NAME: Pied flycatcher

DESCRIPTION: These small, fly-catching birds visit Britain in the summer, after spending winter in Africa. They need plentiful supplies of caterpillars and other insects on which to feed. Males are black with white bellies, while the females are mainly brown. They enjoy singing while perched on tree stumps and dead branches. **POINTS VALUE:** 40

DATE SPOTTED:

WHERE SPOTTED:

SPOT IT!   GOT IT!

NAME: Robin

DESCRIPTION: Adult robins are small birds with red breasts and faces. They are often tame and found in gardens, looking for insects, as well as in woodland. Robins protect their territory fiercely and fight other robins that threaten their home. They eat worms, fruit and insects, and make their nests in any convenient hole or ledge. You can see them all year round, but you will mainly hear them in winter and spring. A high-pitched 'tic-tic' call means that the robin feels alarmed. **POINTS VALUE:** 20

DATE SPOTTED:

WHERE SPOTTED:

SPOT IT!   GOT IT!

NAME: Blackbird

DESCRIPTION: Adult blackbirds are black with orange beaks and yellow circles round their eyes, but female blackbirds are brown with spots on their breasts. They are seen all year round in woodland, farmland and gardens. They stand on grass or soil with their heads cocked to one side, listening for worms below the ground. Blackbirds also eat insects and berries.

POINTS VALUE: 10

| DATE SPOTTED: | SPOT IT! | GOT IT! |
| WHERE SPOTTED: | | |

. . . .

NAME: Starling

DESCRIPTION: Starlings have short tails, pointed heads and triangular wings. They look black from a distance but up close are a mixture of purples and greens. They are noisy and merry, preferring the company of other starlings to being on their own. Flocks of starlings can often be seen sitting on power lines and telephone wires, singing noisily. **POINTS VALUE:** 10

| DATE SPOTTED: | SPOT IT! | GOT IT! |
| WHERE SPOTTED: | | |

NAME: House sparrow

DESCRIPTION: House sparrows build their nests in warm, sheltered hollows in buildings and hedges. They are noisy and cheerful, and can be heard chirping and chirruping all over Britain in towns and in the countryside. Males have streaked brown backs and grey crowns, with white stripes on their wings – females are duller brown. They have adapted to live alongside humans, and eat seeds and scraps. **POINTS VALUE:** 20

DATE SPOTTED:

WHERE SPOTTED:

SPOT IT! **GOT IT!**

· ·

NAME: Chaffinch

DESCRIPTION: Chaffinches can be found all year round. You will usually hear one before you see one as they have a loud song and a 'pink, pink, pink' sounding call. Males are colourful – blue, chestnut, pink and green – whilst the females are generally brown. Both sexes have distinctive wing patterns, which are easy to spot when they are flying. They live in woodland, fields, gardens and hedgerows. **POINTS VALUE:** 10

DATE SPOTTED:

WHERE SPOTTED:

SPOT IT! **GOT IT!**

NAME: Greenfinch

DESCRIPTION: These birds will live anywhere with tall, dense trees and plenty of seeds and insects. They have pink bills and appear as a yellow-green flash when flying. They can often be seen in gardens where there is water, particularly in summertime.

POINTS VALUE: 30

DATE SPOTTED:

WHERE SPOTTED:

SPOT IT!   GOT IT!

NAME: Goldfinch

DESCRIPTION: These finches have bright, red faces and yellow wing patches. They have thin beaks to help them pull out the seeds deep inside thistles – they also enjoy taking scraps from bird tables and feeders.

POINTS VALUE: 50

DATE SPOTTED:

WHERE SPOTTED:

SPOT IT!   GOT IT!

NAME: Bullfinch

DESCRIPTION: Males have bright, pink breasts and pink cheeks, with grey backs and bright, white rumps, making them very colourful and easy to see. Females are not as brightly coloured. Bullfinches eat the buds of fruit trees, often destroying crops. They are found in woodland and in gardens. **POINTS VALUE:** 40

DATE SPOTTED:

WHERE SPOTTED:

SPOT IT!   GOT IT!

DESCRIPTION: Swifts are expert fliers. They collect food and nesting material in flight and drink, bathe, mate and even sleep whilst in the air! They are shaped like a boomerang when flying. They have a tiny bill and are sooty brown in colour, with short forked tails. They visit Britain in the summer from their native Africa. **POINTS VALUE:** 30

DATE SPOTTED: | SPOT IT! | GOT IT!
WHERE SPOTTED:

NAME: Swallow

DESCRIPTION: These small birds have dark, glossy blue backs and red throats. Males have long, streaming feathers, while females have shorter tail streamers. They nest in buildings and under bridges, often returning to the same nest year after year. Nests are made of mud, and bound together with straw. Swallows are thought to be a sign of good luck. **POINTS VALUE:** 30

DATE SPOTTED: | SPOT IT! | GOT IT!
WHERE SPOTTED:

NAME: House Martin

DESCRIPTION: House martins have blue/black upper bodies and white bellies, which can be seen clearly when they fly. They have short, forked tails and small, white feathers covering their legs and toes. They catch insects while flying. They build nests from mud under the eaves of buildings. They spend winter in Africa, and come to Britain in April. **POINTS VALUE:** 30

DATE SPOTTED:	SPOT IT!	GOT IT!
WHERE SPOTTED:		

NAME: Nightjar

DESCRIPTION: They search for food at dusk or dawn. They have pointed wings and long tails, and a soft, grey-brown plumage mottled with a bold, brown marking. This provides good camouflage for them when in their nests on the ground, and when searching for insects and beetles. They also enjoy the occasional moth and can catch them midair by opening their bills very wide. They visit for the summer from Africa. **POINTS VALUE:** 50

DATE SPOTTED:	SPOT IT!	GOT IT!
WHERE SPOTTED:		

25

NAME: Blue tit

DESCRIPTION: Blue tits have blue heads and backs, and yellow chests. They are woodland birds but love to feed on garden bird tables and feeders and nest in boxes. They are very acrobatic and stay together in groups to play and feed. They are often to blame when milk bottle tops have been pecked through when on our doorsteps.

POINTS VALUE: 10

| DATE SPOTTED: | SPOT IT! | GOT IT! |
| WHERE SPOTTED: | | |

NAME: Great tit

DESCRIPTION: Great tits are the largest member of the tit family, and have black heads and yellow and green backs. They are quite aggressive, and fight other tits for food. They like coconut and are happy feeding on husks hung in the garden. They also eat insects, nuts, seeds and household scraps. Great tits live all over Britain in woodland, gardens and parks.

POINTS VALUE: 20

| DATE SPOTTED: | SPOT IT! | GOT IT! |
| WHERE SPOTTED: | | |

NAME: Long-tailed tit

DESCRIPTION: These birds build oval-shaped nests of moss. They have black, white and pink plumage. They are commonly found in woodlands.

POINTS VALUE: 40

DATE SPOTTED:

WHERE SPOTTED:

SPOT IT!   GOT IT!

NAME: Marsh tit

DESCRIPTION: These small birds have black bibs and glossy black caps. Their calls are distinctive 'pitchoo' sounds. They live in beech and oak woods, orchards, gardens and parklands. **POINTS VALUE:** 50

DATE SPOTTED:

WHERE SPOTTED:

SPOT IT!   GOT IT!

NAME: Willow tit

DESCRIPTION: Willow tits have a sooty, black cap extending down the back of their necks, and small black beards under their bills. They have white cheeks and pale grey tummies. They rarely land on the ground, preferring to stay on twigs and branches. They like to build nests in orchards and woodlands. **POINTS VALUE:** 60

DATE SPOTTED:

WHERE SPOTTED:

SPOT IT! GOT IT!

NAME: Skylark

DESCRIPTION: Skylarks are streaky-brown with small crests, which they raise when they're frightened or excited. They have white-sided tails and white edges to the back of their wings that can be seen during flight. They fly vertically into the air, and are very noisy, singing whilst they hover, take off and land – listen out for their distinctive warbling 'chirrup' song. **POINTS VALUE:** 20

DATE SPOTTED:　　　　　　　**SPOT IT!**　　　**GOT IT!**

WHERE SPOTTED:

NAME: Tree pipit

DESCRIPTION: Pipits can be seen during the summer in open woodland, on heaths and downs. They feed on the ground, foraging for insects and spiders. They have brown-streaked upper bodies with buff-streaked chests and flanks. They sing when in flight. They fly high up into the sky and then spread their wings and tails like a parachute and drift down to the ground. **POINTS VALUE:** 40

DATE SPOTTED:　　　　　　　**SPOT IT!**　　　**GOT IT!**

WHERE SPOTTED:

NAME: Pied wagtail

DESCRIPTION: Also known as the 'water wagtails' these birds are often seen near ponds, streams and reservoirs. They are also at home in the countryside, making nests in farmyard buildings and even shallow streams. They have black and white markings and constantly wag their tails up and down. Favourite foods include flies and other insects. **POINTS VALUE:** 30

DATE SPOTTED:

WHERE SPOTTED:

SPOT IT!   GOT IT!

• •

NAME: Grey wagtail

DESCRIPTION: These are elegant black, grey and yellow birds with extra long tails which constantly bob up and down, flashing their yellow underside. Males have black throats. In winter, wagtails roost together in large groups, but are not very sociable during the summer. Nests are built of moss and grass, and are always situated close to fast-flowing water. **POINTS VALUE:** 50

DATE SPOTTED:

WHERE SPOTTED:

SPOT IT!   GOT IT!

NAME: Crossbill

DESCRIPTION: These chunky birds have large heads and their bills cross over at the tips. They are group birds, staying in family units or larger flocks. Males are brick red and females are green-brown in colour. They can be seen all year round, usually in mature forests with lots of pine and spruce trees. They eat seeds from conifer trees, and twitter noisily, making a 'chip chip' call. **POINTS VALUE:** 40

| DATE SPOTTED: | SPOT IT! | GOT IT! |
| WHERE SPOTTED: | | |

- -

NAME: Parrot crossbill

DESCRIPTION: The bills of these birds are very similar to that of a parrot's, and they have sharply forked tails. The males are orange/red with dusky wings, and the females are olive green/grey. They live in pine forests and are very rare. Their distinctive calls sound like a deep 'kop kop' or 'choop choop' noise. **POINTS VALUE:** 60

| DATE SPOTTED: | SPOT IT! | GOT IT! |
| WHERE SPOTTED: | | |

NAME: Magpie

DESCRIPTION: Magpies are scavengers, predators and pest destroyers. Adults have black and white plumage and long tails. Their sides and bellies are white, and their wings are a shimmering mixture of purple, red, blue and green. **POINTS VALUE:** 10

DATE SPOTTED:

WHERE SPOTTED:

SPOT IT!   GOT IT!

NAME: Rook

DESCRIPTION: Rooks have grey/white faces, thin beaks and slightly peaked heads. Their plumage is black with a purple gloss. They have a slow walk and can usually be seen in open fields or grassland. **POINTS VALUE:** 20

DATE SPOTTED:

WHERE SPOTTED:

SPOT IT!   GOT IT!

NAME: Jackdaw

DESCRIPTION: These small birds have grey necks and pale eyes. Their plumage is black. Jackdaws gather in groups, and with other species, in wooded areas such as parkland or on rocks and cliffs. Their favourite nesting place is a hole in a tree trunk. They have a reputation for being thieves, snatching anything they see and can carry. **POINTS VALUE:** 30

DATE SPOTTED:

WHERE SPOTTED:

SPOT IT!   GOT IT!

DESCRIPTION: These large pigeons are seen in the countryside as well as in towns, parks and cities. They are mainly grey with brighter neck and wing patches, which can be seen when they fly. They eat crops like cabbages, peas, sprouts and grain much to the annoyance of farmers, but they also like seeds and berries. Their call is very familiar – 'coo cooooo coo cu cu'. **POINTS VALUE:** 10

DATE SPOTTED: SPOT IT!   GOT IT!
WHERE SPOTTED:

NAME: Collared dove

DESCRIPTION: These doves have browny-pink plumage and black neck collars stretching round the back of their heads. They are usually seen in pairs, feeding on the ground on seeds and grain. They group together round stocks of grain, around barns and farmyards and like to be around people.
POINTS VALUE: 20

DATE SPOTTED: SPOT IT!   GOT IT!
WHERE SPOTTED:

NAME: Turtle dove

DESCRIPTION: Turtle doves are small birds, with chestnut and black speckled backs, black tails and pink breasts.
They have black and white patches on both sides of their necks.
They can be seen during summer in woodlands, hedgerows and parklands. Farmyards are good sources of food for them as they like seeds that have been scattered for the chickens! **POINTS VALUE:** 50

DATE SPOTTED:

WHERE SPOTTED:

SPOT IT! GOT IT!

• •

NAME: Band-tailed pigeon

DESCRIPTION: The band-tailed pigeon can be distinguished from other pigeons and doves by the dark-grey band on its tail. It also has yellow feet, and a black-tipped yellow bill. They like to nest in the branches of tall trees, and feed mainly on acorns. These birds are native to eastern North America, but were exhibited at London Zoo as early as 1949, and you are most likely to see them in captivity. **POINTS VALUE:** 50

DATE SPOTTED:

WHERE SPOTTED:

SPOT IT! GOT IT!

NAME: Kite

DESCRIPTION: These are rare, large birds with small, pale heads and long, forked tails. They have brownish/red feathers and are white under their wings, which you can see when they fly. Kites are most often seen flying over open ground, although they nest in woodland. They eat small animals, birds and insects.

POINTS VALUE: 60

| DATE SPOTTED: | SPOT IT! | GOT IT! |
| WHERE SPOTTED: | | |

NAME: Hen Harrier

DESCRIPTION: Males are pale grey, and females are brown with white rumps and long, striped tails. They are seen during the summer in heather moorland, farmland and river valleys. They eat small animals and birds, and remain silent for most of the time. They are very acrobatic, with males often dropping food from the sky for females to catch. **POINTS VALUE:** 60

| DATE SPOTTED: | SPOT IT! | GOT IT! |
| WHERE SPOTTED: | | |

NAME: Buzzard

DESCRIPTION: These are the most common bird of prey. They have broad, round wings and short necks and tails. Their colours vary between dark and pale brown, and they have pale heads and breasts. The tips of their wings are dark.

POINTS VALUE: 30

| DATE SPOTTED: | | SPOT IT! | GOT IT! |
| WHERE SPOTTED: | | | |

NAME: Goshawk

DESCRIPTION: Their yellow eyes and white eyebrows make these birds look fierce. They have broad wings, long legs and talons that can catch prey while in flight. They live in conifer woods and forests.

POINTS VALUE: 50

| DATE SPOTTED: | | | |
| WHERE SPOTTED: | | SPOT IT! | GOT IT! |

NAME: Sparrowhawk

DESCRIPTION: Adults have grey bodies with stripy red/orange bellies. Females are larger and browner. They have short, round wings and long tails which help them to weave in and out of trees in search of prey. **POINTS VALUE:** 30

| DATE SPOTTED: | | SPOT IT! | GOT IT! |
| WHERE SPOTTED: | | | |

NAME: Kestrel

DESCRIPTION: These birds can often be seen hovering by roadsides, searching for prey in the hedgerows and fields. When they spot food, they hover with their heads still, and drop to the ground in stages before one final swoop to collect their dinner. They eat small animals and birds, and live in Britain all year round. They have chestnut brown backs, and grey heads, and tails. **POINTS VALUE:** 30

DATE SPOTTED:

WHERE SPOTTED:

SPOT IT!   GOT IT!

NAME: Merlin

DESCRIPTION: Merlins, the smallest birds of prey, fly low and fast in search of small birds, insects, lizards and mice. They swoop to the ground and sink their talons into their victim. They have long, square tails and pointed wings. Males are blue/grey with black tail bands, whilst the females are browner. They can be found on moorland, near forests or even by the coast. They make a shrill 'kek kek' sound.

POINTS VALUE: 50

DATE SPOTTED:

WHERE SPOTTED:

SPOT IT!   GOT IT!

NAME: Hobby

DESCRIPTION: Hobbies are dark grey and have black moustaches, short tails and streaked bellies. They can catch small birds or even dragonflies during flight to feast on. Males and females often pass food to each other in midair. They are great travellers and spend the winter in Africa before they fly over 4,023 km to Britain for the summer to breed. **POINTS VALUE:** 60

DATE SPOTTED:

WHERE SPOTTED:

SPOT IT!   **GOT IT!**

. . . .

NAME: Peregrine falcon

DESCRIPTION: These birds occasionally nest on the ledges of high city buildings, but prefer high coastal cliffs. They are aggressive hunters who kill their prey with a strong blow from their talons. They are blue/grey and the tops of their heads are black. They also have black moustaches and big, white eyes. They are swift when flying and chasing their prey, and like to eat other birds, including pigeons. **POINTS VALUE:** 50

DATE SPOTTED:

WHERE SPOTTED:

SPOT IT!   **GOT IT!**

NAME: Golden eagle

DESCRIPTION: Often called the King of Birds, golden eagles are huge brown birds with golden-tinged head feathers, and flat foreheads and beaks. They hunt in pairs in the winter for birds and animals, and can lift a fox from the ground before carrying it away. They live in nests in moorlands and mountains, and hunt over open fields where they can easily spot prey. **POINTS VALUE:** 50

DATE SPOTTED:

WHERE SPOTTED:

SPOT IT!   **GOT IT!**

NAME: Osprey

DESCRIPTION: Seen from below, ospreys have white bellies and dark, speckled backs. Their heads are white, with brown eye streaks running from their beaks to the back of their necks. They eat fish, and are at home around freshwater rivers in the summer. They hover over the water before plunging in to catch their prey. In winter, they fly to western Africa. **POINTS VALUE:** 60

DATE SPOTTED:

WHERE SPOTTED:

SPOT IT!   **GOT IT!**

NAME: Honey buzzard

DESCRIPTION: Honey buzzards have narrow heads and long tails that fan out behind them. They can be found in the summer near woodland or forests. **POINTS VALUE:** 60

DATE SPOTTED:

WHERE SPOTTED:

SPOT IT!　　**GOT IT!**

. . . .

NAME: Barn owl

DESCRIPTION: Barn owls have heart-shaped faces, with buff backs and wings and pure white bellies. They live in open country, especially in farmyards with barns, and also like marshland. They hunt at night. **POINTS VALUE:** 40

DATE SPOTTED:

WHERE SPOTTED:

SPOT IT!　　**GOT IT!**

. . . .

NAME: Snowy owl

DESCRIPTION: The adults are almost pure white, flecked with dark brown, although the female has heavier brown markings. They have bright, yellow eyes and small, curled beaks. In flight, they glide like buzzards, before pouncing on their prey. They are almost extinct in Britain, so seeing a snowy owl is very rare. **POINTS VALUE:** 60

SPOT IT!　　**GOT IT!**

DATE SPOTTED:

WHERE SPOTTED:

NAME: Little owl

DESCRIPTION: Little owls have long, musical calls that can often be heard on spring evenings. They can be found around farmland and in farmyards, parkland, old orchards and quarries. In daylight they can be seen perched on a tree branch or telegraph pole. They have speckled, brown bodies with yellow eyes, and wear a 'frowning' expression. Small animals, birds, beetles and worms are their favourite foods. **POINTS VALUE:** 50

| DATE SPOTTED: | SPOT IT! | GOT IT! |
| WHERE SPOTTED: | | |

NAME: Tawny owl

DESCRIPTION: These large owls have round bodies and heads, rings of dark feathers around their faces and huge, dark eyes. They are red/brown in colour with pale bellies. They can be seen all year round in woodland, farmland and gardens. They make 'hoo hoo oo hoooo' sounds. **POINTS VALUE:** 50

| DATE SPOTTED: | SPOT IT! | GOT IT! |
| WHERE SPOTTED: | | |

NAME: Long-eared owl

DESCRIPTION: Ear tufts make these owls easy to identify. They often look long and thin, and raise their ear tufts when they are alarmed. They are brown with darker streaks, and have deep orange eyes. Active only at night, these owls spend the day roosting in dense tree cover. They live in woodland, farmland and moorland, and eat small rodents and birds. **POINTS VALUE:** 60

DATE SPOTTED:

WHERE SPOTTED:

SPOT IT! GOT IT!

NAME: Short-eared owl

DESCRIPTION: These owls have mottled brown bodies and big yellow eyes. They can be seen hunting in daylight or at dusk just above the ground. They use their ears to pinpoint movement and noise in the undergrowth to signal where food can be found, such as voles and mice. Nests are built on the ground in open areas near moorlands and heaths where food is plentiful. **POINTS VALUE:** 30

DATE SPOTTED:

WHERE SPOTTED:

SPOT IT! GOT IT!

41

NAME: Pheasant

DESCRIPTION:
Pheasants are large, long-tailed birds. Males have rich chestnut backs and dark green heads with red faces. Females are mottled black and pale brown. They can be seen in woods, fields and hedgerows, and by the side of country lanes. **POINTS VALUE:** 20

| DATE SPOTTED: | SPOT IT | GOT IT! |
| WHERE SPOTTED: | | |

NAME: Red grouse

DESCRIPTION: These birds have dark, red/brown plumage, and striking white legs. Above each eye is a bright red 'eyebrow', called a wattle. They take off from the ground vertically, and then level off before flying away. Nests are built in shallow hollows that are well hidden in heather or other moorland vegetation.
POINTS VALUE: 40

| DATE SPOTTED: | SPOT IT! | GOT IT! |
| WHERE SPOTTED: | | |

NAME: Black grouse

DESCRIPTION: Males are all black with red eyebrows, and have a streak of white across their wings that shows when they fly. They have fanned tails with white feathers underneath. Females are smaller and grey-brown with smaller, forked tails. **POINTS VALUE:** 40

DATE SPOTTED:

WHERE SPOTTED:

SPOT IT! GOT IT!

NAME: Partridge

DESCRIPTION: Males have distinctive brown horseshoe marks on their breasts, and have grey necks and breasts and orange faces. When flying, their tails fan into a semicircle of orange feathers. They live in the countryside near woods and forests. **POINTS VALUE:** 30

DATE SPOTTED:

WHERE SPOTTED: SPOT IT! GOT IT!

NAME: Quail

DESCRIPTION: Quails are small, stocky birds striped brown and cream, and have orange bellies. They don't like flying and like to remain hidden in tall vegetation, in meadows and woodland.

POINTS VALUE: 60

DATE SPOTTED: SPOT IT! GOT IT!

WHERE SPOTTED:

43

NAME: Grey budgerigar

DESCRIPTION: These budgies are grey/yellow in colour, with grey feet and small beaks with blue patches on top of them. Their fluffy head feathers give these birds a comical, appealing look. They make fun pets as they are sociable, easy to look after, and can sometimes learn tricks and a few words. They like to eat seeds, fresh vegetables and cereals. **POINTS VALUE:** 10

DATE SPOTTED:	SPOT IT!	GOT IT!
WHERE SPOTTED:		

NAME: Border fancy canary

DESCRIPTION: These birds are bright yellow with white feathers in their wings. Their tails are long and their beaks broad and pointed. Colours can vary – you can find green, white and cinnamon-coloured canaries too. They love to sing, and enjoy splashing around bathing. Fruit and green foods are their favourites, though they also like eggs. **POINTS VALUE:** 10

DATE SPOTTED:	SPOT IT!	GOT IT!
WHERE SPOTTED:		

NAME: Gloster fancy canary

DESCRIPTION: These rare canaries are easily identified by the beautiful crest of feathers on the top of their heads that looks rather like a mop! They have thick necks, and yellow and white chins under small pointed beaks. Their bodies are speckled brown and black, with white and pale yellow bellies. They live for around ten years.

POINTS VALUE: 60

DATE SPOTTED:

WHERE SPOTTED:

SPOT IT! GOT IT!

• •

NAME: Celestial (Pacific) parrotlet

DESCRIPTION: Theses are tiny parrots, not much bigger than the size of an adult's hand, and are quite happy living in a small space. They are mainly green, with blue feathers under their wings, and have small, pink beaks and pink feet. They eat seeds and fruit. Sometimes these birds can be very argumentative, so they are usually kept in pairs rather than large groups. **POINTS VALUE:** 30

DATE SPOTTED:

WHERE SPOTTED:

SPOT IT! GOT IT!

45

(**NAME:** Blue-headed parrot)

DESCRIPTION: These beautiful parrots have vivid yellow and green bodies, and blue heads. Their eyes are huge and black, surrounded by white. Their bills can vary in colour and often look flaky. This is due to wear and tear and is nothing to worry about. With training, these parrots love to chatter away, and make good companions. **POINTS VALUE:** 30

(**DATE SPOTTED:**) (**SPOT IT!**) (**GOT IT!**)
(**WHERE SPOTTED:**)

· ·

(**NAME:** Blue-crowned hanging parrot)

These parrots got their name from the unusual way that they roost, hanging upside down from their perch. They are best homed in an aviary rather than a small cage as they can be very messy eaters! They are green with blue patches on the top of their heads, and have red throats and tail feathers. Like most parrots, they eat seeds and fruit. **POINTS VALUE:** 40

(**DATE SPOTTED:**) (**SPOT IT!**) (**GOT IT!**)
(**WHERE SPOTTED:**)

NAME: Senegal parrot

DESCRIPTION: Senegal parrots have yellow bellies and beautiful green throats and wings. Their heads are grey, their beaks hooked and broad, and they have bright yellow eyes. **POINTS VALUE:** 30

DATE SPOTTED:

WHERE SPOTTED:

SPOT IT!

GOT IT!

NAME: Masked lovebird

DESCRIPTION: Usually housed in pairs, lovebirds are small and stocky with very friendly temperaments. They are green with red beaks and white eyes, and their heads are dark brown/black. They are noisy and like to entertain themselves by stripping bark from branches. **POINTS VALUE:** 40

DATE SPOTTED:

WHERE SPOTTED:

SPOT IT!

GOT IT!

NAME: Cockatiel

DESCRIPTION: Their distinctive yellow crests on the top of their heads stick up vertically when these birds are excited. They have yellow faces and orange cheeks, and grey bodies. They are very sociable birds, and like to mix with other species.

POINTS VALUE: 30

DATE SPOTTED:

WHERE SPOTTED:

SPOT IT!

GOT IT!

47

Index

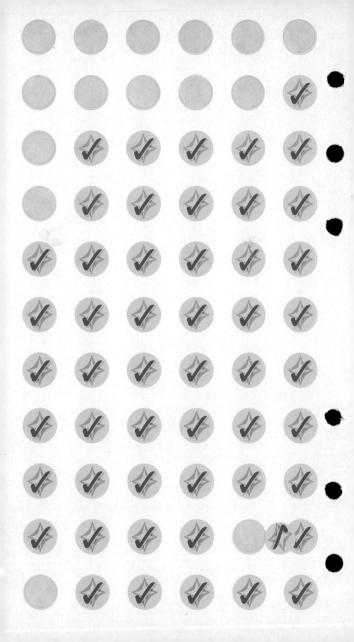

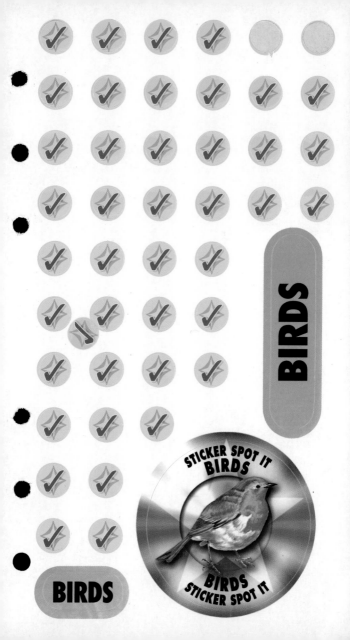

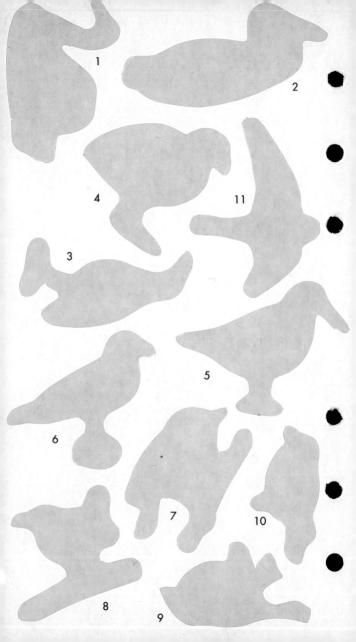

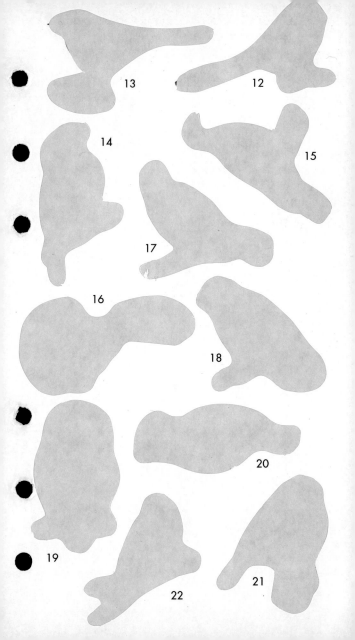